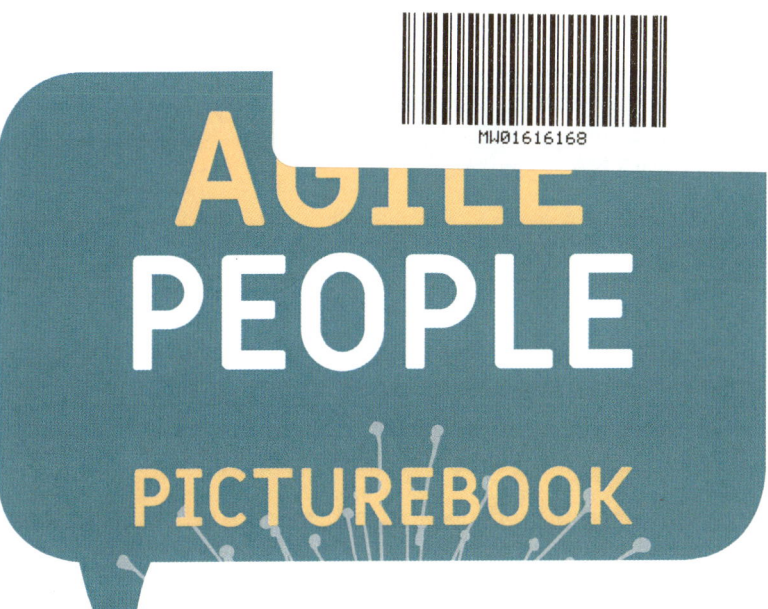

AGILE
PEOPLE
PICTUREBOOK

Preamble

Don't let the light format of this excellent book fool you. Although this is an easy and fun read, the topic is dead serious. There is a crisis in how we lead and organize work today.

Our organizations are not designed to keep up with today's complex and rapid changing demands. Nor are they fit for people.

This is reflected in low scores in engagement surveys around the globe and the challenge to attract, grow and develop talent, especially the younger generation. They have totally new expectations of their work experience. They demand highly engaging cultures, a compelling purpose, opportunity to have a positive impact and continuous growth throughout their career.

This book will give the overview and introduction to all the Agile People concepts you need to set you off on a journey towards an agile organization, more fit for people and the future.

Michael Göthe,
Agile Organizational Coach at Crisp

Table of content

The future belongs to organisations that embark on the journey of adapting to the environment and releasing their employees potential

Chapter 1
Introduction

To ensure teams are well crafted, motivated, and successful, leaders must adapt to new ways of working and thinking - they must become agile.

We need to accelerate an agile mindset by spreading the values of customer collaboration, energized people, learning organizations, inspiring leadership, and rapid change.

The Agile People Picturebook is a spin-off project from the book called "Agile People - A Radical Approach for HR and Managers (that Leads to Motivated Employees)". It summarizes Agile People and the main messages from the book in pictures and quotes and is a joint effort between me and Nico and Elsa Simpson.

I first met with Nico and Elsa on a trip to South Africa in November 2018 when I was giving training in Cape Town. They helped to make this book come alive with the drawings and quotes and is an easy and fun read that will help people to understand the why, what and how of change for the future of work.

Pia-Maria Thoren

In the struggle for survival, the fittest win out at the expense of their rivals because they succeed in adapting themselves best to their environment

The Darwinian hypothesis; civilisations past & present

Survival of the fittest

Choosing to adapt
Where have we actively chosen to adapt in the past?

Agile People Mission

There is a shift happening in the world of work. Organisations are becoming more inspiring, human, and purposeful. Organisations that are fit for humans and the future. Business is becoming a force for good.

Peoples potential is freed up to have a positive impact on people's lives, community, and the world.

Our purpose is to accelerate this transformation by spreading the agile values of customer collaboration, energised people, learning organisation, inspiring leadership, and rapid change to all areas of business and organizations.

AGILE PEOPLE MANIFESTO

Agile People are curious and collaborate **to** create awesome value and innovative solutions that meet human needs
(Engagement, Innovation, Curiosity)

Agile People actively embrace diversity and inclusion **to** create communities where people feel safe and truly belong
(Diversity, Safety, Belonging)

Agile People connect deeply with individuals, businesses and society **to** create a culture where human ability is nurtured, valued and unleashed
(Culture, Connection, Humanity, focus on broader society)

Agile People continuously pursue meaning and purpose in life **to** create a positive and significant impact in the world of work
(Purpose, Meaning)

Agile People actively seek opportunities to experiment and learn **to** adapt fast and thrive in a changing environment
(Adaptability, Experimentation)

Agile People promote transparency across organizations and teams **to** enable trust, ownership and self-organisation
(Transparency, Commitment, Accountability, Self-organisation)

Agile People harness the power of boundary spanning **to** facilitate proactive collaboration across organizational barriers
(Cross-Functional, Collaboration, Communication, Learning)

The Agile People Manifesto was crafted in a gathering in Smögen, Sweden, in June 2019 by 19 agile people from 15 countries all over the world

Bala Asirvatham, Cheryl Tansey, Claudio Lingua, Ed Cadura, Gustavo Couto, Helgi Gudmundsson, Inanc Civaz, James Stone, Kjell Tore Guttormsen, Michele Stone, Mikael Leinsköld, Ola Berg, Pablo Delgado, Pan Wei Ng, Pia-Maria Thorén, Steve Conard, Tamara Molinas, Wouter Bak, Åsa Holmberg

Chapter 2

Agile principles

"Agile is a MINDSET, a way
of thinking, and a collection
of values around how work
should be organised in
a complex and
ever-changing world"

Critically, agile is not a method - it is a way of thinking according to a set of values.

Agile is a mindset.

Agile is a mentality that allows people and groups to meet challenges, learn quickly, and respond to change.

Incremental approach

What would it mean for us to take an incremental approach, work in small batches and then evaluate?

How can we structure our work to complete small batches or sprints, and then evaluate and test?

Agile is a MINDSET, a way of thinking, and a collection of values around how work should be organised in a complex and ever-changing world.

Agile mindset

How do we tap into the human potential for creativity?

Trust-based management

How can we use experimentation and trust-based management to increase our employee engagement and ensure longevity in the marketplace?

If you are not clear on the organization's why, the employees won't be either.

Innovation happens everywhere

Are we solely relying on a few at the top or a specific department for innovation?

Within a sustainable system, working becomes both a challenge and a reward.

You are securing a future by constantly innovating.

Continuously reward and encourage organically formed teams

"What is the next step I can take to make our dream a reality?"

Waterfall presupposes that the world is predictable, which it categorically is not.

Waterfall Method is an antiquated approach that does not suit the pace of change in today's world.

The failure rate is extremely high because we cannot control change and change is a reality.

> The Waterfall approach requires extensive pre-planning and zero deviation from the plan.

Waterfall model

Do your time-lines and project phases allow for shifts in the marketplace or customer feedback?

In 2001, a group of IT professionals met at a ski resort in Utah and wrote the Agile Manifesto and the Twelve Principles:

"We are uncovering better ways of developing software by doing it and helping others do it.

Through this work, we have come to value:

Individuals and interactions *over*
processes and tools

Working software *over*
comprehensive documentation

Customer collaboration *over*
contract negotiation

Responding to change *over*
following a plan

"That is, while there is value in the items on the right, we value the items on the left more"

The Twelve Agile Manifesto Principles

These principles describe a culture in which change is welcome, and the customer is the focus of the work.

1. Customer satisfaction through early and continuous software delivery

2. Accommodate changing requirements throughout the development process

3. Frequent delivery of working software

4. Collaboration between the business stakeholders and developers throughout the project

5. Support, trust, and motivate the people involved

6. Enable face-to-face interactions

7. Working software is the primary measure of progress – Delivering functional software to the customer is the ultimate factor that measures progress

8. Agile processes to support a consistent development pace

9. Attention to technical detail and design enhances agility

10. Simplicity – Develop just enough to get the job done for right now

11. Self-organizing teams encourage great architectures, requirements, and designs

12. Regular reflections on how to become more effective

Twelve Principles of the Agile Manifesto

1 Satisfy
the customer

2 Welcome changing
requirements

3 Deliver working
products frequently

4 Collaborate
daily

5 Motivated
individuals

6 Face-to-face
conversations

7

Measure of progress
through working products

8

Promote sustainable
development

9

Continuous attention to
technical excellence

10

Simplicity
is essential

11

Self-organizing
teams

12

Regularly reflect on
continuously improving

Agile strive for fewer processes, systems, reports, and checklists. They gobble up management's time and energy.

Function like a network

Do people have the freedom to act locally, make decisions quickly, and communicate freely with others and customers in real time?

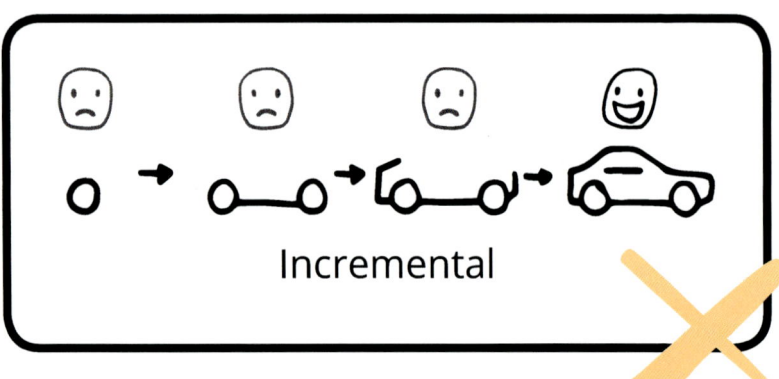

Incremental

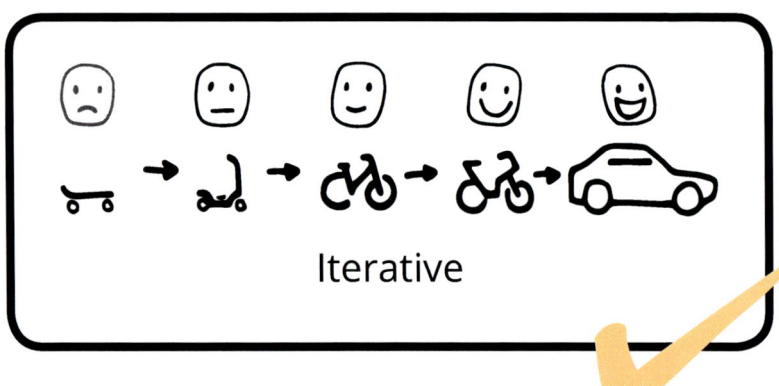

Iterative

Originally described by Henrik Kniberg

The only true reality is that we must adapt to survive.

Real-time feedback needed

Do you assume that you do not know and cannot plan for what will happen in the future?

Smaller pieces mean delivering faster and creating value as early as possible for customers.

Breaking work down into smaller pieces

Do we satisfy customers through continuous value delivery?

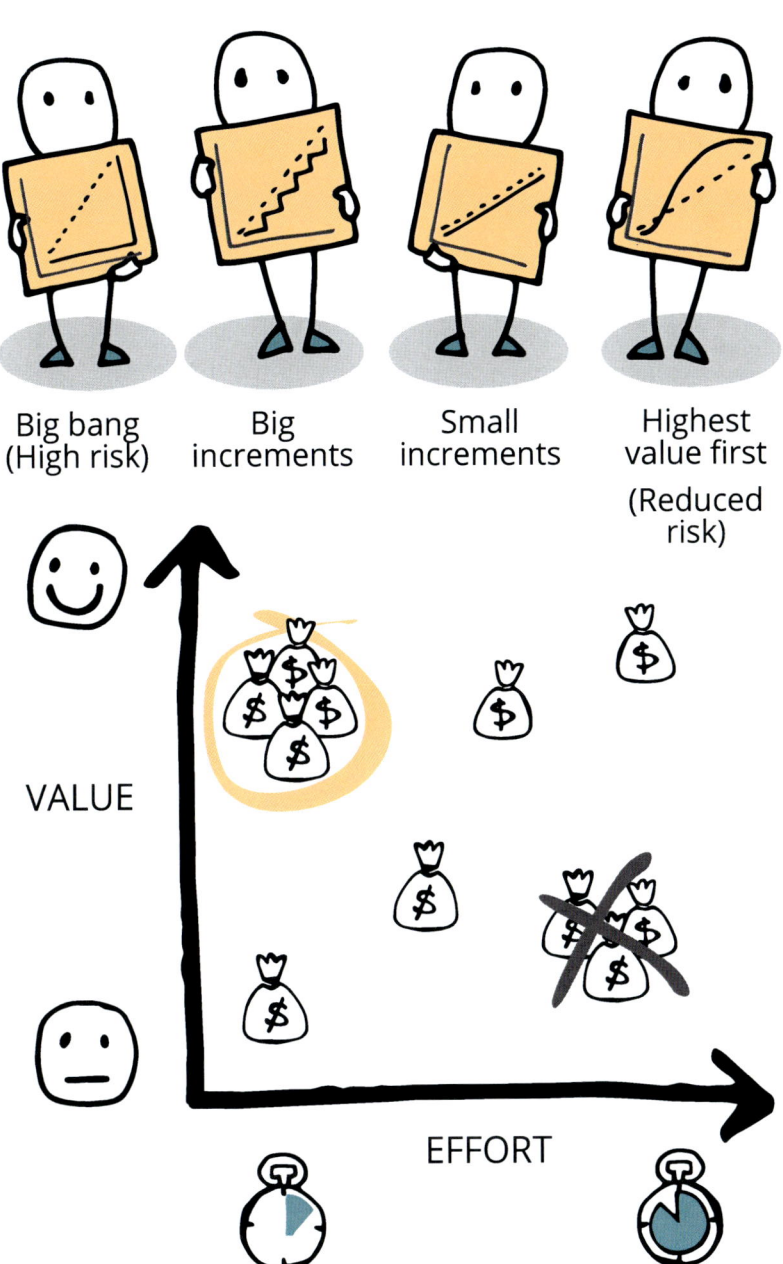

Big bang
(High risk)

Big
increments

Small
increments

Highest
value first

(Reduced
risk)

VALUE

EFFORT

Aim for the highest value first

Less bureaucracy

① Functional team creating business value

② Scrum daily

③ Collaborative planning and review

④ Return to incremental development

Agile is about being able to adapt to change - specifically, the changing needs of the customer.

The company must understand what creates the most value for the customer and strive to deliver it above all else.

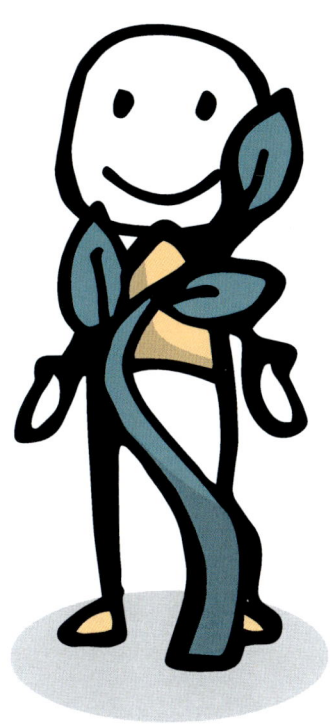

Continuous learning and improvement

Autonomy in the workplace means that individuals can control their own workflow without being micromanaged.

They can make their own choices and decisions about what to work on, where to focus their energy, and what they need to learn.

Autonomy leads to less stressed employees and teams.

Autonomy

People are working remotely with increasing frequency. They must be trusted to organize their time and get their work done in alignment with the rest of their team and organization.

It starts with trusting people

Diverse organizations tend to experience superior output, and it's easier to achieve diversity when people feel secure.

It's also much easier to deal with change when people are comfortable with each other.

Relatedness

The sense of injustice, or perceived unfairness, always stems from a comparison with someone else.

Fairness

Do you act like a good gardener, creating an environment that supports growth and provide the prerequisite that supports abundance?

There is no universal solution for handling the pace of change, but agile is the way to work for the future.

Agile Maturity Pillars

Motivation
To make an organization hum, you need to start with the people.

Areas of change
If you want to be agile, ask:
Is there value in everyone working in the same way?

Leadership & culture
Creating those good circles where the culture and the structure reinforce an strengthen each other.

Structure
What changes can be made to support less management and more collaboration?

For agile to be successful, you need to come to the stage where you are not only using tools - you have also changed your mindset and work with new principles and a new set of company values that will come gradually from your new agile culture.

Chapter 3
Agile organizational structures

"How we view other people will affect how we structure our management processes"

Pia-Maria Thoren

Everyone is yearning for a better way to work together.

Soulful workplaces

Are you creating a workplace where people's skills and talents meet their deepest desires?

A company can thrive when it has the right blend of structure and chaos, which is in between over-structured and complete disaster.

A little bit of structure is necessary to focus on productivity and creative work, but too much structure stifles creativity.

"This is what we want to do, this is how far we need to go, and these are our limitations."

Aligning constraints

Do people know the why behind what they do, and do they know the rules of the game?

Hierarchical Organizations

Do you use a one-way,
top-down, silo approach?

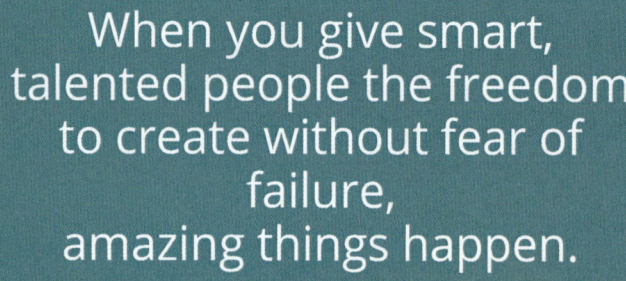

When you give smart, talented people the freedom to create without fear of failure, amazing things happen.

New employees are brought in to add value to the company; it's up to them what they do with the opportunity and what role they will play.

Flat Organization

Does your organization acknowledge that communication has no regard for hierarchy?

People will always talk and share ideas with each other, regardless of the managerial structure.

In real life, communication flows like a network.

Knowledge will soon be the only competitive advantage, so the companies that can learn and adapt fast are the ones that will survive.

Hyper-innovative and creative

Fit between VALUES and STRUCTURE

If we trust someone -
why detailed reports?
If we value creativity and innovation -
why detailed, limiting job descriptions?

If we want cooperation -
why reward individual performance?

If we want to engage the whole self -
why numerical targets?

If we imagine equality -
why promote only some?

If diversity is important -
why so few women in top management?

Do you have a fit between the culture
(values and behaviour) on the one hand
and the structure (methods, processes,
and systems) on the other hand?

Agile is a seismic mindset-shift.

"The key to success lies in an organization's ability to adapt to change."

Self-steering Nodes

Freedom to act locally
Make decisions quickly
Communicate freely in real time
Function like a network
Always moving, changing and adopting

The best solutions come from working cross-functionally.

Many to many

How can we provide the best structures to allow people to give their best efforts?

> We need to learn how to allow people to give their best effort to the company by enabling supporting structures to emerge.

Design structures

Manage the system, not the people?

Modern Agile
(Joshua Kerievsky)

Make people awesome

Deliver value continuously

Make safety a prerequisite

Experiment and learn rapidly

Modern agile is like a
lighthouse that offers guidance
and illuminates the path.

Fear is the greatest roadblock to creativity.

Abolishing
the culture of fear

Are we creating an environment where people feel comfortable enough to make wild suggestions, to say what's on their minds, and to experiment without judgement or penalty?

Switch to a structure that focuses on customer value over rules and policies.

If the business demands change and adaptability to new customer needs, fixed processes are not the answer.

Customer value

How can we enable people closest to the issue to be the ones making the decisions?

Reinventing Organizations
Frederic Laloux

Wolf Pack

Constant exercise of power by chief to keep troops in line.

Fear is the glue of the organization.

Highly reactive, short term focus.

Thrives in chaotic environment

Mafia

Street Gangs

Terror Organizations

Division of Labour

Command authority

Army

Highly formal roles within a hierarchical pyramid.

Top down command and control (what and how).

Stability valued above all through rigorous processes.

Future is repetition of the past.

Catholic Church

Military

Governmental Organizations

Public School System

Formal roles (stable and scalable hierarchy)

Processes (long term perspectives)

Machine

The goal is to beat the competition; achieve profit and growth.

Innovation is the key to staying ahead.

Management by objectives (command and control on what; freedom on the how)

· Multi-national companies

·Charter Schools

· Innovation

· Accountability

· Meritocracy

Family

Within the class pyramid structure, focus on culture and empowerment to achieve extraordinary employee motivation

· Culture Driven Organizations

·

Empowerment

· Values-driven culture

· Stakeholder model

Network

No one is the boss of anyone else.

Hierarchy is not powerful enough to face complexity, e.g., global economy, human muscle brain (cells).

If you take your purpose seriously, there is no competitor by definition

· Network Organizations

· Self Management

· Wholeness

· Evolutionary Purpose

Teal Organisations

are complex, participatory,
interconnected, interdependent,
and continually evolving systems,
like ecosystems in nature.

Teal organizations

Primarily self-organizing,
decentralized networks.

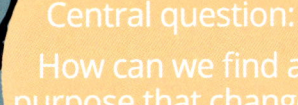

Central question:

How can we find a
purpose that changes
and develops?

Running a business today is less about the process than it is about people, teams, and relationships.

The word 'process' alone indicates control

How can we do performance management and learning without trying to fit it into a process?

Culture eats everything ~~strategy~~ for breakfast!

Chapter 4
Agile HR

"Traditional performance
management causes people
to focus on all the
wrong things"

If we change the way our HR processes work along with our mindset, we obviously shape a different culture.

Fabiola Eyholzer

Manifesto for Agile HR Development

We are uncovering better ways of developing an engaging workplace culture by doing it and helping others do it.

Through this work, we have come to value:

Collaborative networks over hierarchical structures

Transparency over secrecy

Adaptability over prescriptiveness

Inspiration and engagement over management and retention

Intrinsic motivation over extrinsic rewards

Ambition over obligation

That is, while there is value in the items on the right, we value the items on the left more.

CHANGE change c change change h change change a change CHANGE aha ChinGEchange ang ong

Central group HR can support the shift towards agile through:

Support flexibility, speed, and collaboration

Involve the customer in delivery

T-shaped HR people who can take on many different roles

Teamwork (cross-functional)

Value stream based HR

Playing many different roles

Stable, high performing teams

Salary formulas and profit sharing (can be performance related)

Supporting the organization to perform

No-size fits all

Experimentation

Human view Y

When HR managers hold on to traditional ways of working, learning, developing, and planning, they are severely reducing the possibility for change

Lightweight and flexible

Are we focusing on customer value over rules and policies?

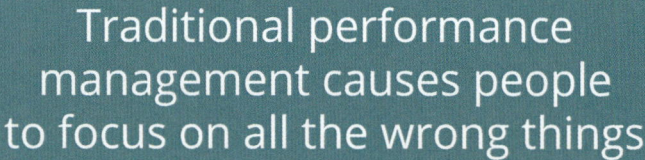

Traditional performance management causes people to focus on all the wrong things

Annual performance goals and ratings are often completely out of sync with agile initiatives and goals.

Focus on strengths

How can we focus on strengths instead of weaknesses when evaluating performance?

IMPROVED EMPLOYEE PERFORMANCE

Set and revise goals

What do I need to learn?
What competencies are necessary
to reach our goals?

Plan for development

Establish several small goals to make
it easy to change course.

Lead, serve and coach

When goals are achieved,
the agile start again.

Follow up

Share feedback and
celebrate successes

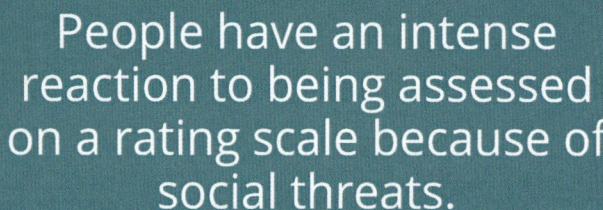

People have an intense reaction to being assessed on a rating scale because of social threats.

When goals are tied to finances or status, sandbagging often occurs.

Bonus systems promote self-optimization.

Sandbagging means setting lower goals so they can be achieved more easily.

People put their own individual goals ahead of the team, creating an unhealthy competitive environment.

How can we get our annual performance goals and ratings in sync with our agile initiatives and goals?

Use several smaller sessions throughout the year.

Be transparent to the rest of the team.

Allow the employee to decide on the structure of the conversation.

Open improvement conversations

How can we focus on improvement for the future, rather than judging the past?

Four phases of team development:

1 Polite and tiptoeing

2 Squabble and conflict

3 Calm and find a place

4 Focus on productive work

In uncertain situations:

1 We can't know
what will happen.

2 We need everybody's brains
to try to figure out the
best way forward.

3 Acknowledge your fallibility -
you are not perfect.

4 Ask many questions.

5 Show that you don't
have all the answers.

Well-functioning teams do more for each other than they do for themselves.

One plus one equals three

Do you replace conflicts with constructive discussions to focus on the same goal?

Teams cannot achieve their goals unless its members are capable enough to complete the necessary tasks and experiment to find solutions.

Learn to succeed

Are you ensuring that everyone learns what they need to learn to succeed?

What do you think was your greatest achievement?

What do you think was your biggest mistake?

What do you think you need to change to stay motivated and perform?

How do you think you have progressed toward your ambitions?

What could I, as a manager, have done to support you better?

What are your ambitions for the next period?

Feedback session guidelines

The value of ongoing conversations is immeasurable.

General salary rule:
Market-based and fair

Compensation

Are we paying enough
to get the salary issue of the table?

Ladder

Jungle gym

Workplace

A salary discussion doesn't have to poison the water at work.

Intrinsic motivation

When the secrecy surrounding the topic is removed, there is a universally positive impact on trust, motivation, and culture.

SALARY FORMULA
(Jurgen Appelo)

Develop criteria for what
is important to reward

Weigh all the factors
against each other

Develop a formula to
calculate a salary that is perceived
as fair as possible by as many
people as possible.

Do NOT use bonuses as rewards.

Big rewards and bonuses have been proven to decrease performance and increase stress. Keep the rewards small and distribute them often.

Give unexpected rewards

Do we celebrate accomplishments in public?

Whenever something has been accomplished, regardless of how large or small, it should be accompanied by a celebration.

Giving recognition

Do we make it easy for co-workers to reward each other?

Celebrations serve to reinforce learning and good practices and give people a sense of belonging and togetherness.

Look for reasons to celebrate.

Does your reward system emphasize teamwork and de-emphasize money?

Hire for attitude; train for skill.

Large organizations tend to get mired down in bureaucratic red tape and nonsensical hiring criteria.

Small team approach

Are you looking for people who will complement your company and who will add to your team?

It might be more important to look for drive and passion than the right competencies.

In some cases, motivation is the most important quality.

People can learn a lot

"Can you do the job?"

Person's strengths and weaknesses

"Will you love the job?"

What motivates someone

"Can we work with you?"

Persons fit in the team

If an employee from your organization encounters someone who embodies the company values, that person should be brought in to meet the team and assess how they can contribute to the company.

Always recruiting

How do you include the team in the decision-making process; and, at the end of the day, how do you make sure that the team has a say?

Be transparent with information on the company website and make it easy for people to learn about what you stand for and value.

Attraction starts with branding

How are we as a company positioned in the marketplace?

Transparency is key.

A simple and flexible approach to the hiring
process is ten times more effective than
a rigid, step-by-step program.

We need people who are self-directed and collaborative.

Don't hire jerks!

Do your managers lead in a way that releases motivation in others so they can function optimally?

The point is to allow people to
work when, where, and
how they work best.

When people go to work,
they shouldn't have to leave
their hearts at home.

Betty Bender

Employee engagement:

An equation between personal satisfaction and organizational contribution.

Happy employees lead to happy customers, which leads to happy profit margins and the fulfilment of the company's higher purpose.

Gallup
"State of the Global Workplace" Q12®

Questions

1. I know what is expected of me at work.

2. I have the materials and equipment I need to do my work right.

3. At work, I have the opportunity to do what I do best every day.

4. In the last seven days, I have received recognition or praise for doing good work.

5. My supervisor, or someone at work, seems to care about me as a person.

6. There is someone at work who encourages my development.

7. At work, my opinions seem to count.

8. The mission or purpose of my company makes me feel my job is important.

9. My associates or fellow employees are committed to doing quality work.

10. I have a best friend at work.

11. In the last six months, someone at work has talked to me about my progress.

12. This last year, I have had opportunities at work to learn and grow.

Engaged employees feel connected to their companies. They go to work with passion and enthusiasm. They drive innovation and move the organization forward.

Engaged employees

With connectivity at an all-time high, working remotely is the reality for today's corporations.

The younger generation of employees expect flexibility and choices when it comes to where and how they work

Flexibility and choices

Do you understand that the current workforce is global, connected, mobile, transient, and multi-generational?

The younger generation expects that they will be able to work when, where, and how they desire.

The current workforce expects workplaces that are transparent, dynamic, specialized, interconnected, and performance driven.

The world is moving towards a border-less existence, meaning people are no longer confined to their offices.

Autonomous Workforce

Can your workforce work anywhere, any time of day or night, and however they choose?

If career paths are needed (which is not obvious), they should be as flexible as possible.

Succession planning

Is it possible to move up, down, out of your organization and then back in again to another function that fits the circumstances of employees?

Chapter 5

OKRs

"Objectives and key results help to unify the whole company towards one common direction"

Ideas are precious,
but they're relatively easy.
It's the execution that's everything.

John Doerr

To step towards the future, build a goal model centred on creating customer value in everything the company does.

How can I make creating customer value our central principle and use it as a guidepost for decision making?

ALIGNED AUTONOMY

High autonomy
People decide HOW
to reach their goals.

High alignment
People are moving
in the same direction.

For goals to be effective, they need to be inspiring.

inspire *

Goal-setting

If you want engaged employees and a culture of exploration and experimentation, the goals must have some pizazz.

Do our goals convey a sense of excitement and purpose?

Sandbagging is when employees establish low-performance targets so they can more easily meet their goals and receive a bonus.

Sandbagging fosters a culture of mistrust.

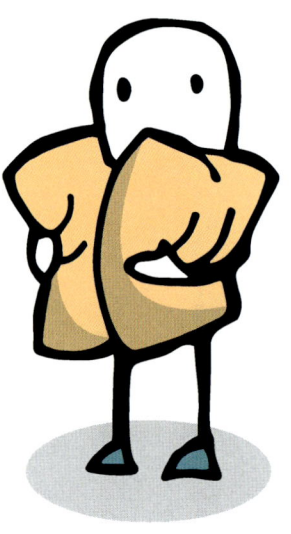

Sandbagging

Employees do as little as possible, and managers squeeze them to death.

Objectives and key results help to unify the whole company towards one common direction.

Objectives and key results

Are our OKRs connected, transparent, progress-based, adaptable, and aspirational?

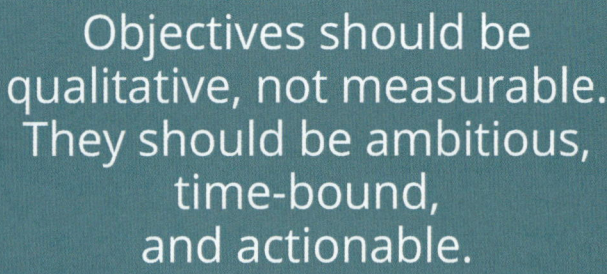

Objectives should be qualitative, not measurable. They should be ambitious, time-bound, and actionable.

Objectives are stretch goals

Do our objectives require stepping outside of the comfort zone?

Key results should be based on outcomes, not tasks, and they should focus on where the employee is now and where they want to be in the future.

YES!

Key results are extremely measurable.

Are you focusing on outcomes - what you are trying to achieve - rather than activities?

Focus on improving in a common direction.

Do NOT use OKRs for appraisals or bonuses. It spoils the concept of trust and honest conversations.

Chapter 6

Learning & Development

"Failure is simply a part of constant learning"

The only competitive advantage that remains is knowledge, continuous learning, and innovation.

The company that learns the fastest and transforms the learning into new products and services will have a competitive advantage.

Learning as a lifelong process

The most pressing task is to teach people how to learn.

Drucker

The whole organization benefits from nurturing all people to better themselves.

Building internal knowledge and skills leads to faster innovation

When people learn as a team, they have the opportunity to reach group goals faster and easier.

Continuous organizational learning

Do you innovate by focusing less energy on trying to achieve perfection and more energy on accepting mistakes?

Shorter work cycles and project retrospectives are an effective strategy for overcoming the fear of action.

Team learning starts with dialogue.

Stop making assumptions and interact on a real level

Organizations are dynamic systems in a state of continuous adoption and improvement.

Fail fast

Are you creating an open environment, where experimentation is encouraged, making mistakes are acceptable, and different viewpoints are welcome?

We need cross-functional, interdisciplinary, continual, self-directed formal and informal education.

Learning is a never-ending process.

People learn most effectively in small chunks.

Invite to mingle

Are you creating environments that invite people to communicate and mingle?

People who develop a broad and general competence base with deeper knowledge in particular areas.

Broad Generalist

Focused Specialist

T-shaped people

> T-shaped people mean increased flexibility because they can swap tasks and try on several different hats.

Decreasing bottlenecks

Are people able to work together in small, shifting, and evolving teams?

Job descriptions are boxes to stand on, not live in

Develop in any direction as long as it benefits the whole organization.

Are your job descriptions foundations for growth instead of restrictions?

Lunch and learn
facilitates quick learning

Do people use their lunch hour to
exchange ideas and try out new things?

Having a partner helps
to make people more
accountable to themselves,
their buddy,
and the company.

Pairing

Do people pair up to design, test, manage,
or simply explore new ideas together?

Self-education is, I believe, the only kind of education there is.

Isaac Asimov

The people who have extensive knowledge in a particular area are considered an "informal leader."

When team goals change, so does the informal leader.

Tomorrow's companies embrace continuous learning and development as an investment

Chapter 7

Psychological safety

"Where there is trust, there is autonomy, and where there is autonomy, there is productivity"

There are many situations where, if people felt psychologically safe and asked the right questions, mistakes could be avoided.

Psychological Safety

Psychological Safety

We are not afraid to...

Be ourselves

Make mistakes

Ask questions

Take risks

Raise problems

Disagree

Where there is trust, there is autonomy, and where there is autonomy, there is productivity.

The experience of social pain, while temporarily distressing and hurtful, is an evolutionary adaptation that promotes social bonding and, ultimately, survival.

Naomi Eisenberger

Social pain

Do you remember that employees experience organizations as a social system, not as a system designed for economic transactions?

Chapter 8
Agile Leadership

Modern leaders face a dual challenge. There is a way we collaborate in groups and teams.

The way leaders can lead is framed by those that follow them... in what ways do we like to follow?

The plain fact is that we do not like to follow leaders whose approach is based on control and command anymore. What we like to follow is instead based on principles like agency, contribution, transparency, delegation, and inclusivity.

Organisations seek increased agility at all levels, then the need for more collaboration, more teams, and better teamwork also increases.

The need for effective leaders becomes more important than ever before. In effect, the role of the team leader becomes one of the most important in the whole organisation. As leaders, it's time to elevate our game. Its time to become an enabler, someone who support and clears the way to make it possible for people and teams to collaborate, produce, thrive, and be happy at work.

That is what Agile Leadership is about.

Helgi Gudmundsson

Agile People Coach & Facilitator

Agile leadership...

... is about people: empowering them, letting them take control of decision making, choosing effectiveness, doing the right thing, and setting the direction.

...is about focusing on tasks, speed, efficiency, good practices, and helping teams direct their energy and activities productively.

It is not practical or realistic to assume that an entire company can be managed from a control tower.

Delegate decision making

Are you a company of self-steering nodes?

Human view X

1. Dislikes work and will avoid it

2. Must be forced or bribed to put in effort

3. Lack ambition and dislike responsibility

4. Motivated by money and job security

5. Lacks creativity and resist change

Human view Y

1 Driven by job satisfaction

2 Actively seek work

3 Show ambition and seek responsibility

4 Motivated by a desire to realize your own potential

5 Creative and ingenious

One of the reasons some people are resistant to agile is because it levels the playing field. Control and power are spread democratically throughout an organization.

Replacing the concept of 'boss' with self-management

You manage things;
You lead people

Admiral Grace Murray Hopper

Traditional company structures date back to the command and control model.

Your team is an organic system, not a machine

Are your management and HR processes built on distrusting people?

Agile leadership is brain-friendly leadership.

It nurtures the parts of people's psyche that allows them to operate at the highest level of functioning while avoiding circumstances or interactions that cause people to shut down

> The goal of agile leadership is to delegate as much power as possible to the employees.

Bottom-up approach

Are leadership informal and do communication flow freely between everyone?

New leaders

Lead a community full of internal social activists

Drive a cause with volunteers

Guide a social movement of brokers

Broker peer-to-peer networks with widespread teaming up

Invest in business campaigns

Compile opinions and ask people

Live non-negotiable behaviour on the ground

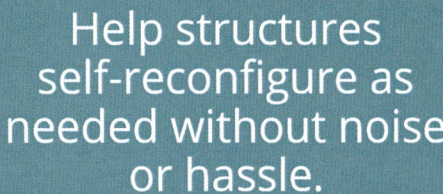

Help structures self-reconfigure as needed without noise or hassle.

Speak human language

Love their work

Make a visible impact

We cannot predict what is going to happen or when. It all depends on the relationships, the people, the system, the structures, the processes, and the organization itself.

Support complete transparency

Do you look at the whole picture?

Continuous improvement requires continuous learning and the opportunity to experiment and make small, calculated mistakes.

Improve everything all the time

Are you always looking for ways to get better across all channels?

The seven levels of delegation
"Delegation Poker" from Management 3.0

1. Tell

2. Sell

3. Consult

4. Agree

5. Advise

6. Inquire

7. Delegate

We have to unlearn jumping in and telling people what to do. We have to stop dictating what people are supposed to do, and instead, work on empowering them.

The Gmail story proves that good things happen when you allow people to relax into their creative head-space.

It's a more productive approach than having employees fill out forms, adhere to checklists, and constantly report on their progress.

When there is trust, there is no need for constant reporting anyway. The only reason for all the reporting is to maintain control, and in agile management, control is distributed.

Managers need to focus their activity on keeping people actively and creatively engaged and motivated.

Energize people

Leaders who fear powerlessness fail to understand they are not dealing with a zero-sum game.

Holding on to an 'I win, you lose" mentality does not serve the greater good of the team or company.

Managers become more powerful once they give power to others, or delegate responsibility.

When power is distributed, we all win.

Is the fundamental anchor of your team, trust?

CEO
=
Chief Enabling Officer

Chapter 9

Engagement

"Motivation can only come from within. It is triggered by people's inner drive and desire to make something happen"

People behave differently when they know they are working towards a higher purpose that supports a shared dream.

1. Create better engagement:

Find a dream with the power to unite.

2. Create better engagement:

Have fun at work

Do you create opportunities for laughter and camaraderie?

The culture of control is hindering employee engagement and performance.

The tighter the reins, the less control management actually has.

3. Create better engagement:
Empower people

A culture of transparency serves to replace many of the policies and rules that would otherwise exist.

Don't underestimate the power of peer pressure, which has more sway in a group setting than an unspoken expectation.

4. Create better engagement:

Create an environment of transparency

Most people want to know how they're doing and if their work is valuable. Feedback gives them the wings to fly.

5. Create better engagement:

Provide feedback

The perks of providing feedback are that it can be delivered quickly, it's free, and its impact has a lasting positive effect.

6. Create better engagement:

Use constructive criticism

Winning teams know how to regroup and redirect their attention to the vision and mission that support the dream.

7. Create better engagement:

Keep a laser-like focus

If someone does their best thinking after midnight, so be it. If someone wants to work from a remote jungle and Zoom into team meetings - that's fine too.

8. Create better engagement:

Create a high degree of freedom and flexibility.

Quality suffers
when people have too much
on their plate.

Motivation can only come from within. It is triggered by people's inner drive and desire to make something happen.

We need our businesses to
create a culture where it's easy
to be committed and positive,
where it's easy to understand
the company's overall goals,
and how the team and
I can help to achieve them.
And, where I feel respected,
listened to, and valuable.

Measure engagement with three questions:

1. What feels best right now?
2. What feels the worst right now?
3. What can you or your boss do to increase your satisfaction?

Chapter 10
Agile tools & practices

"The idea is that you can deliver a product according to plan, shorten the lead-time, and communicate faster and clearer by focusing on one task at a time"

Dealing with work in small batches is a common practice in agile

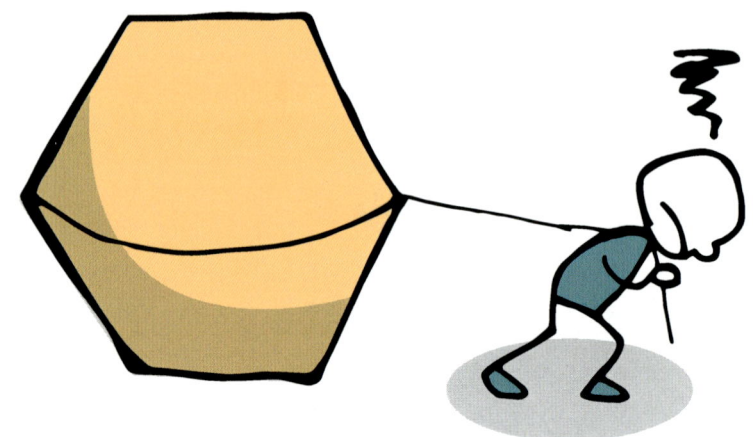

Deliver all at once

Deliver in bite-sized sections

> The brain loves visualizing through pictures, models, and drawings.

Visualizing where you are

Do you enhance understanding by using visuals to create consensus?

Foster an environment of experimentation

Scrum

The idea is to reduce complexity and focus on building products and services that directly meet the customer's needs.

Providing value for the customer is the primary goal and transparency, evaluation, and continuous improvement is built in the form of daily stand-ups and retrospectives.

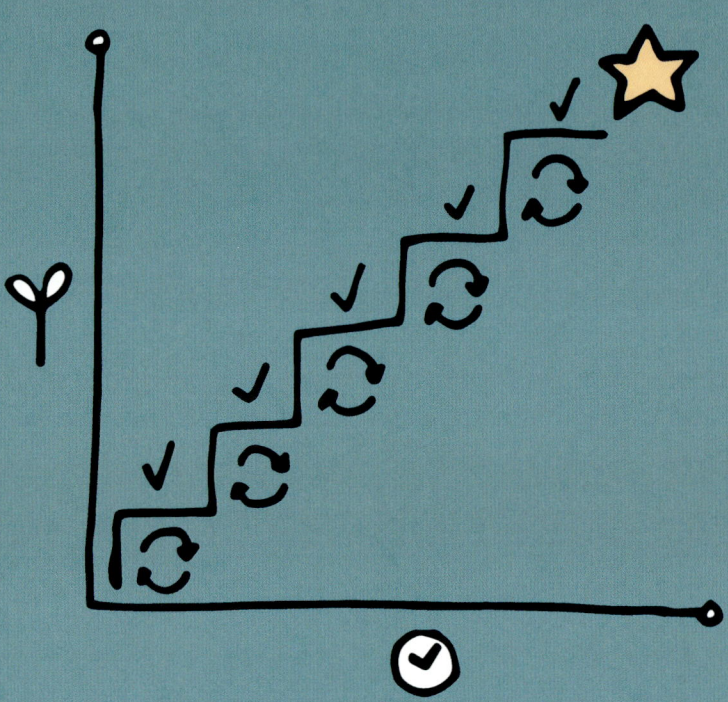

Short work cycles ensure constant improvement, quick learning, and encourage listening to and utilizing customer feedback.

The team decides how work is performed and tasks are dispersed.

Work is accomplished fluidly

Do all team members share responsibility for the results of their efforts?

The product owner owns the product backlog, which is a list of features, goals, or to-do items that constantly shift based on the feedback from various stakeholders.

Product owner

Product owners are also responsible for the overarching vision for the product, so they make sure the development team is working on the right initiatives.

Scrum teams conduct sprint-planning meetings.

DISTRACTION

SCRUM MASTER

Scrum master

Are you making sure that the team isn't disturbed or distracted while working on a sprint?

The daily stand-up meeting requires 100 percent transparency and vulnerability, which takes a lot of courage.

Daily stand-up meetings

Are your stand-ups quick and efficient and never last longer than fifteen minutes?

Once the sprint is over, the team presents the result to the customer in a sprint demo meeting, where the customer gives feedback that goes into the backlog.

Sprint demo meeting

The minimum viable product is the least possible 'thing' that a team can deliver to the internal or external customer that creates some sort of value.

Minimum viable product.

At the end of each sprint, the team meets to examine what worked and what didn't.

Sprint retrospective

Do you look for areas that can be improved, changed, or introduced between sprints?

User stories identify the WHO, the WHAT, and the WHY behind projects.

User stories

Are you using your product backlog as a resource for high-level, bare-bone user stories?

Scrum is not an ad hoc tool; it's a very focused way of approaching work.

Scrum

Do you use a fixed structure and a specific procedure?

The idea is that you can deliver a product according to plan, shorten the lead-time, and communicate faster and clearer by focusing on one task at a time.

* Signboard or billboard" in Japanese

KANBAN*

Do you promote better communication through visual project management?

DUE   TO DO   DOING   DONE

The advantages of agile

High visibility through project cycles due to the use of daily stand-up meetings.

Shorter feedback loops are leading to reduced risk and increased learning.

Dividing work into sprints allows the organization to deliver value regularly to the customer and get results faster.

Continuous customer contact through real-time demos allows for immediate solutions to complex projects.

The SCARF Model

David Rock - 2008

Status – our relative
importance to others.

Certainty – our ability to
predict the future.

Autonomy – our sense of
control over events.

Relatedness – how safe we
feel with others.

Fairness – how fair we
perceive the exchanges
between people
to be.

Humans are biologically programmed to care about status because social acceptance impacts the ability to survive. It's much easier to exist in the pack than out on your own as a lone wolf.

No lone wolf

Most employees in large organizations learn how to handle criticism and hard to swallow information. They become 'transactional employees' who only give what they feel they are getting in return.

Transactional employees

Everyone on the team must adopt a management mindset to take care of the organization and make decisions that will have the best possible outcome for it.

'To manage' from the Italian word maneggiare, to handle and train

Management is too important to be left to the managers!

Jurgen Appelo

Positive feedback triggers the status section of the brain. It doesn't require a large reward; only a small display of appreciation is enough to tap into that section of the brain.

Positive feedback

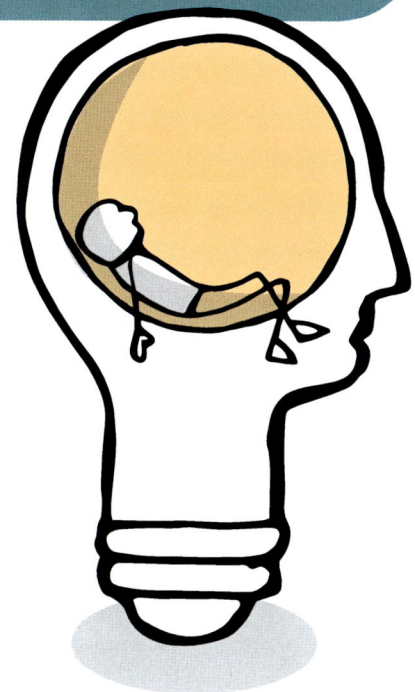

Familiar situations allow the brain to relax and go into autopilot.

Being in uncertain situations requires extra energy and focus on coping.

Certainty

When handling uncertainty, do you break it down into smaller, more manageable pieces?

To decrease feelings of uncertainty surrounding an obstacle, managers and a leader should make all related information as transparent as possible.

Transparency makes coping with uncertain situations less stressful.

Chapter 11

System & Complexity

"The future belongs to companies that embark on the journey of adapting to the environment and releasing their employees' potential"

One of the big misconceptions is that agile organizations have no structure, no bosses, and no documentation - the very picture of anarchy.

In fact, agile organizations have the ability to both create change and respond to it. They are constantly balancing between flexibility and stability.

Complexity comes into play when dealing with people and relationships. People are not predictable, so you don't know exactly what's going to happen next.

High degree of uncertainty

> Everything happens at once across all channels and can't be governed by a single, central authority.

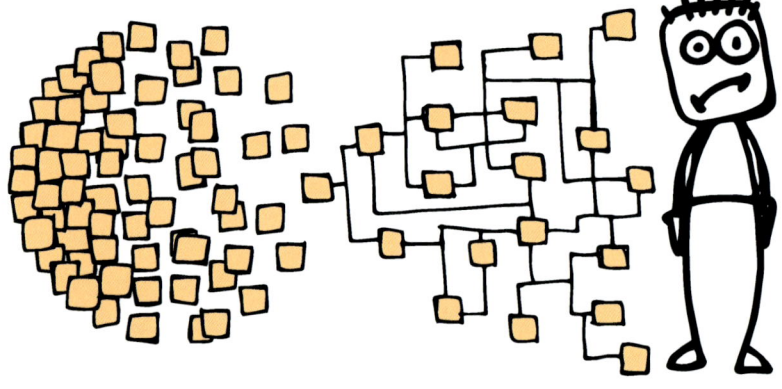

Complex systems are more than the sum of their parts.

Do you spread governance among all the parts?

Complex systems tend to be spontaneous, disordered, and vibrant, especially on the brink of chaos.

Complexity theory

In chaotic times
do something
and see what
happens

Marielle Heijltjes

Agile is suitable in complex situations and actually prevents them from tipping over into anarchy.

The future belongs to companies that embark on the journey of adapting to the environment and releasing their employees' potential.

Chapter 12
Graphic facilitation

The illustrations in this book have been done by our friends and partners
Nico and Elsa Simpson.

Their belief in a graphical way of explaining "anything", is in this last chapter explained more in detail

We hope that you enjoyed reading this book and see that "serious" matters can be explained in a more interesting way

Action megaphone

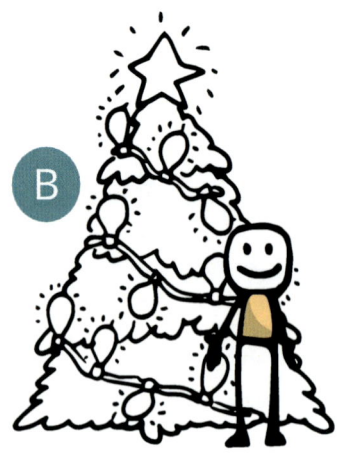

Light up the brain

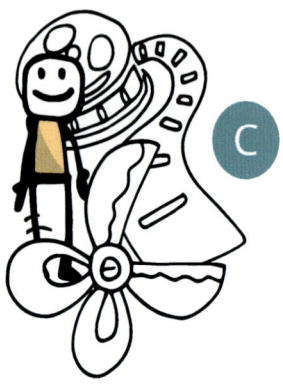

Cut to the chase

Diversity

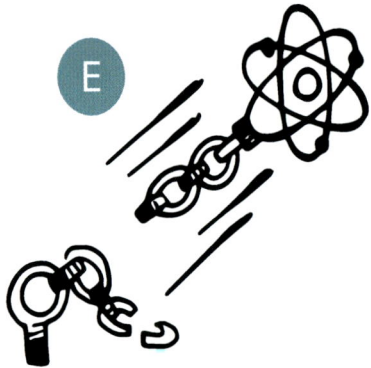

Unchain the energy

Funnelling knowledge

The a-z
of graphic facilitation

Graphic facilitation is a way of using concept illustrations that facilitates the process, captures the insights and moves the group forward through graphic illustrations.

Ⓐ Action Megaphone

A visual process analysis acts like an action megaphone. It clarifies which actions are important and urgent to take. It motivates people to self-organize around the vision and work collectively towards a common goal. A clear visual process becomes a source from which all sustainable and
consistent action flows.

Ⓑ Light up the brain

The illustrations capture the rational as well as emotional content of the process. This light up participants brains 'like a Christmas tree."

Ⓒ Cut to the chase

A visual process 'cuts' directly to the 'chase." It is a short-cut to big picture insights and a common map of understanding. This accelerates innovation and efficiency.

Ⓓ Diversity

Graphic Facilitation can enable effective communication with diverse groups, no matter how big the group. It can do this because it uses a variety of learning styles and accommodates different levels of literacy and abilities.

Ⓔ Unchain the energy

Sometimes one needs a fresh method of communication to unchain the energy of a group. Graphic Facilitation concentrates the people, securing focus through catching their ideas. This leads to synergy and have an energizing impact on team awareness, drive, and organization.

Ⓕ Funnelling knowledge

To understand complex information at a glance a group must generate creative ideas and then funnel this knowledge into a work plan. A Graphic Facilitator can help people see what they currently know - without taking sides. When the group see what they are thinking it almost always helps them 'get their head around' fussy situations.

Getting on same page

Record hidden insights

Innovative metaphors

Juxtaposed juggling

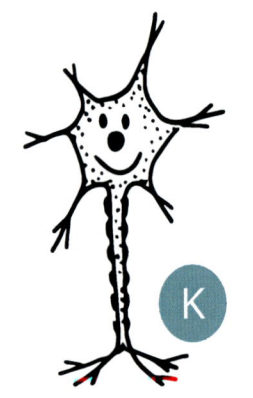

Explicit knowledge

Listen on meta level

Ⓖ Getting on the same page

Often groups have trouble getting on the same page. Leaders then need to help people get clarity and get focused. They want to facilitate understand for one another and work through difficulties and group dynamics. The point is to focus a groups understanding and figure out what to do.

Ⓗ Record hidden insights

Illustrating a person's thoughts increase everyone's focus and clarity. It is an effective way to open up and record deeper understanding and hidden insights. When you 'draw' on the wisdom of all the people in the room it opens up more profound insights and lead to better decisions.

Ⓘ Innovative Metaphors

Metaphors can unleash new thinking. Visual metaphors generated by a group often enlighten and lead to innovative new ideas.

Ⓙ Juxtaposed juggling

To understand business processes companies need juxtaposed ideas and juggle contradictions so nothing is lost or overlooked.

Juggling insures that subtle relationships are honoured and not only shown in a linear format. Juxtaposing helps with seeing the big picture and the details simultaneously.

Ⓚ Explicit Knowledge

Graphic Facilitation is a type of explicit group recall. It is a way to capture the views of participants in real time and making this knowledge available to the whole group.

Ⓛ Listen on meta level

For groups to move forward leaders need to help them move beyond the group politics and listen on a meta level – deep listening. The visual representation catalyses dialogue and invigorates thinking during meetings.

Ⓜ Multifaceted Problem solving

Solving complex problems requires that we use the perspectives and creative insights of diverse people. Visual illustrations are an effective tool for capturing the complexity of the problem and promoting healthy way of thinking.

Multifaceted problem solving

New cards

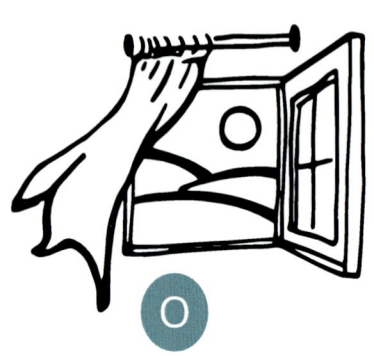

Open window

Project/product planning

Quickened communication

Real time consensus

Ⓝ New cards

Graphic recording captures the emerging thinking and dynamic process of the group when minds meet. It steps up and boosts group efforts and ultimately produces 'new cards.'

Ⓞ Open a window

Rich pictures help open windows on situation that carries a degree of complexity. Rich pictures show relationships, perspectives, action, time, journeys, and vision.

Ⓟ Project and product planning

Some scientific research has shown that visual language can shortens meeting time by almost a quarter. It aids in the decision making process, and assists in planning and implementation.

Ⓠ Quickened Communication

A plain visual story can help communicate your ideas in a clear, gripping and quick way. The illustrated information can easily be shared afterwards, making the meeting easily to grasp and rapidly promotes the free flow of ideas across an organization.

Ⓡ Real time Consensus forming

For consensus forming a groups needs rapid, in-real-time synthesis of ideas and processes When participant's ideas are drawn out in real time the group not only stays on topic but conflicts are also minimized as the group sees the equal presentation of multiple perspectives.

Ⓢ Sparking fresh ideas

By returning to our visual roots, and realizing images are integral to sparking innovation we help groups be innovative and spark fresh ideas. The process combines a world based on words and numbers and a world where insights are based on the metaphoric images.

Ⓣ Thinking made tangible

Seeing our thoughts illustrated in a tangible way help us face complex multi-faceted problems. Build refined systemic understanding and brings broad strategic insight.

Ⓤ Unlocking Understanding

Graphic Facilitation unlocks participant's ability to voice their understanding. While the audience watch and engage in its creation participants can add and recognize their own Aha! Moments.

Sparking fresh ideas

Tangible thinking

Unlocking understanding

Visual flow

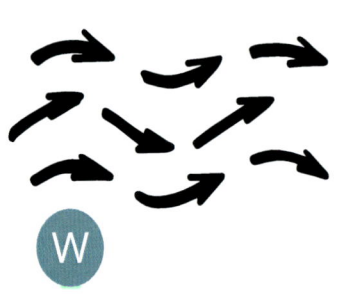

Whole-brain engagement

Xploratory playfulness

Ⓥ Visual Flow

Images, illustrations and symbols, colours, pictures and groupings become a visual flow of the 'as is' scenario. This becomes the background upon which the group can imagine an improved process.

Ⓦ Whole-brain engagement

Graphic facilitation uses imagery as a way of drawing out group thinking, helping groups "see what they mean". The use of imagery combined with structure kindles whole-brain engagement.

Ⓧ xploratory Playfulness

Concept illustrations help groups break new ground, probe, prospect, scout, search, examine and inspect. All this is done in a cheerful, joking, light-hearted, lively and playful way.

Ⓨ Yield a conceptual map

Visual images can catalyse the discussion in a group and supply a common map of the issues in question from which people can move forward with a shared sense of understanding,
ownership and purpose.

Ⓩ Zooming in on gaps

Paradoxically seeing the big picture help groups zoom in on the gaps in the process. Visual plotting help groups to discover and name these process gaps without getting bugged down in the detail.

Yield a map

Zooming in on gaps

Illustrations by Nico and Elsa Simpson

Agile People Picturebook

ISBN 978-91-519-2211-9 Paperback

ISBN 9789151922119

Made in the USA
Coppell, TX
30 April 2021

54813838R00128